Remembering My Grandparent

A KID'S OWN GRIEF WORKBOOK IN THE CHRISTIAN TRADITION

Nechama Liss-Levinson, PhD
Rev. Molly Phinney Baskette, MDiv

Walking Together, Finding the Way®
SKYLIGHT PATHS®
PUBLISHING

Remembering My Grandparent:
A Kid's Own Grief Workbook in the Christian Tradition

2006 First Printing
© 2006 by Nechama Liss-Levinson and Molly Phinney Baskette

Library of Congress Cataloging-in-Publication Data

Liss-Levinson, Nechama.
Remembering my grandparent : a kid's own grief workbook in the Christian tradition /
by Nechama Liss-Levinson, Molly Phinney Baskette.
p. cm.
ISBN-13: 978-1-59473-212-6 (hc)
ISBN-10: 1-59473-212-4
ISBN-13: 978-1-68336-259-3 (pbk)
1. Death—Religious aspects—Christianity—Juvenile literature.
2. Bereavement—Religious aspects—Christianity—Juvenile literature. 3. Grief—Religious aspects—Christianity—Juvenile literature. 4. Grandparents—Death—Juvenile literature. I. Baskette, Molly Phinney, 1970–   II. Title.

BV4906.L57 2006
248.8'66—dc22

2006018544

Cover design: Sara Dismukes

SkyLight Paths Publishing is creating a place where people of different spiritual traditions come together for challenge and inspiration, a place where we can help each other understand the mystery that lies at the heart of our existence. SkyLight Paths sees both believers and seekers as a community that increasingly transcends traditional boundaries of religion and denomination—people wanting to learn from each other, *walking together, finding the way.*

SkyLight Paths, "Walking Together, Finding the Way" and colophon are trademarks of LongHill Partners, Inc., registered in the U.S. Patent and Trademark Office.

Walking Together, Finding the Way®
Published by SkyLight Paths Publishing
A Division of LongHill Partners, Inc.
An imprint of Turner Publishing Company
4507 Charlotte Avenue, Suite 100
Nashville, TN 37209
Tel: (615) 255-2665
www.skylightpaths.com

This Book Belongs To

_____

This Book Is about My

_____

This Book Was Given to Me By

_____

In celebration of my mother-in-law,
Sylvia Levinson,
known to everyone as "Grandma Sylvia."
—Nechama Liss-Levinson

To our family's grandparents-in-training:
Grampa George, Mamgu, Granny Wendy, Gramma Susan, and Kathleen;
and to the memory of Grampa Jim, who had time to love Rafe
before leaving us.
—Molly Phinney Baskette

Acknowledgments

This book is written for all children, but when I write, I think about my own children, Rivka and Bluma, my son-in-law, Jeff, and my future grandchildren. When Rivka and Bluma's grandparents, Grandma Bubbles and JoJo, and Grandpa Aaron, died many years ago, my daughters helped me to understand what kids think and how they feel.

I have received love and support from friends and family, including my Florida sisters, the Wednesday lunch diner group, my walking buddy, and the rest of the usual suspects. I want to thank my husband, Billy, for being my lifetime best friend and touching my life forever with his good heart, beautiful voice, and helping hand.

I could not have written this book without my writing partner, Reverend Molly Baskette. She brought great ideas, good humor, and lots of fun to the job of being an author. I thank Stuart M. Matlins, the publisher of SkyLight Paths, for deciding to publish this book, and Mark Ogilbee, for being so very helpful and nice as our editor.

Finally, I thank God for all my blessings.

—Nechama Liss-Levinson

Deep love and gratitude go to my husband, Peter, the "memory detective" who has searched me out, heart and soul, and to my best fren', Sarah, for making me laugh when I feel like crying. Thanks to my beloved son, Rafe, whose nighttime questions and worries opened up the child's inner world for me, and my daughter, Carmen, who was born at the same time as this book.

I want to thank Nechama Liss-Levinson, whose wonderful book for Jewish children first inspired me to work on this project; Stuart M. Matlins, publisher of SkyLight Paths; our editor, Mark Ogilbee; and my supportive and loving congregation, First Congregational Church of Somerville UCC.

And, finally, thanks to the children who first made me a "mother," and their honorary Grandpa: the boys and girls of the Casa San Jose Orphanage in Colima, Mexico, and Padre Francis Welsmiller, who taught me how to hold life joyfully and death gently.

—Molly Phinney Baskette

Contents

What This Book Is About and How to Use It: A Message for Parents

If you have picked up this book, it probably means that one of your parents or in-laws recently died, or is expected to die. This is a difficult transition for children and adults alike. We all have complex reactions to death. What does it mean for us that this person died? Who will die next? What is the meaning of our life and its end here on earth?

It can be doubly challenging when we as parents are confronted with the questions and experiences of our children in the face of our own grief. How are we to protect our children and keep them feeling safe, while teaching them important lessons about the nature of the world and our place in it?

At times like this, we can turn to deep spiritual traditions and practices for comfort and help in answering these questions. This book combines the wisdom of the Christian faith with the teachings of psychology to assist you in helping your children learn to grieve with less anxiety and more honesty. The activities in this book cover the various stages of grieving and speak to the challenges your child may face throughout the year following the death of a grandparent.

Your child will be offered the opportunity to remember his or her relationship with the deceased grandparent and place this transition within the natural cycle of life and death that faces all of us. There has been an attempt to present difficult concepts, including death, burial, cremation, soul, resurrection, spirit, and charity in ways that are both honest and accessible to children. There are numerous activities presented in this workbook to help your child integrate these ideas, including reading, writing, drawing pictures, asking questions, and making collages.

This book is best used when a parent and child initially look at it together. Your level of involvement with the projects will depend on the age and personal inclinations of your child. But as your child goes through the book, a special moment in time opens up for you to talk with them about your own parents, your values, and the mysteries and miracles of life and death.

Don't be afraid to have these amazing conversations, and to answer the tough questions, even if sometimes the truest answer may be, "I'm not sure." Take this opportunity, amidst your own grief, doubts, and questions, to grow in spiritual connectedness to your child. We hope that this book will become a treasure that your child will continue to use and return to for spiritual comfort and joyful memories in the years ahead. This hands-on book that you and your child create together will enrich your family in ways you can't yet imagine.

What This Book Is About and How to Use It: A Message for Kids

If you are reading this book, something sad probably happened in your family. One of your grandparents died. It may have been your grandmother. It may have been your grandfather.

This is your book. Unlike most other books, you can write in this one. You can draw, doodle, take notes, tape in pictures, and even fold the pages.

 Begin by writing the name of the person who died:

_____

You might be wondering what happens when someone or something dies. All living things have a beginning and an end. Flowers start out as seeds, grow into big blooms with beautiful colors, and then one day die. Little kittens are born, grow up into playful cats, and, over time, grow old and die. God created the world this way.

All people are born as babies. As we grow, we learn to smile and crawl, and then to walk and to talk. When we get old, our bodies get old too. One day our bodies stop working, and we can't eat or drink, walk or talk, or even breathe. This is called dying.

You can have so many different feelings when someone dies. You might be sad, angry, mixed-up, or scared. At times you may not feel anything at all. Your feelings might be going up and down like a roller coaster. One minute, you want to cry, and then you just don't feel like crying. You might feel unexpected things, like wanting to act silly, or to laugh a lot.

Sometimes, kids might even feel guilty about things they did, or for feelings they had about their grandparents. Some kids might feel glad that their grandparents aren't sick anymore. Some kids are worried about their parents, or about a grandparent who is still alive.

What are some of the ways you have been feeling?

_____

_____

_____

This book is to help you during the whole year after your grandparent dies. The first part is a special section with things to do right before and after the funeral. The second part has activity pages you can use later on, any day of the year. And the third part can help you think about your grandparent during the holidays. You can fill out the pages in the order they're written, or you can skip around. There may be some pages you don't want to do at all. That's okay. It's up to you.

You may have a lot of questions about what happened and about what's going to happen in the future. This book will help you answer some of those questions and encourage you to go to your mom or dad to ask more questions. This is a book to help you remember your grandparent who died. As you fill in this book, you will be creating a special treasure that you can keep forever.

Draw a picture of your grandparent who died. (You can draw from memory or use a photograph to help you.)

part one
Remembering after the Funeral

When someone we love dies, the world may suddenly seem upside down. You don't know what to do or what to say. Our Christian tradition helps us to feel less mixed up by giving us special instructions on "what to do" after someone in our family dies. This section has some activities to help you in that special time after the funeral.

About the Funeral

When someone you love dies, life can seem very confusing for a while. In the Christian faith, after someone dies, there is a funeral, a special service where ministers or priests, friends, and family say prayers and tell stories about the person who died. Each story told at the funeral is called a "eulogy," which means "good word." After the funeral, your grandparent's body, which may be lying in a beautiful box called a coffin, can be buried at a special park called a cemetery. Sometimes, the body of the person who died is turned into ashes, using a special fire. This is called "cremation," and the ashes are put in a favorite place that your grandparent loved, such as near the ocean or the mountains. Sometimes, the ashes are kept in a special container in a cemetery or other place where the family can visit.

Some families gather the day before the funeral at a funeral home. Usually, the body of the dead person is at the funeral home too, all dressed up and lying in the coffin, looking a little like they're just sleeping, even though the person is dead, not just sleeping. This time together is sometimes called a "wake," even though the dead person will not wake up. It is also called a "viewing" or "visiting hours." During this visit, friends and family talk about the happy times and the sad times they've shared with each other and with the person who died.

For the day or two before or after the funeral, family and friends may visit you at home (or at another relative's house) and bring food for your family to eat. They will look at family pictures, say special prayers, or tell stories about your grandparent who died. Often, kids don't know what to do during this time, and feel kind of left out. Some kids who felt close to their grandparents miss them a lot, and aren't sure how to handle those feelings. Other kids didn't know their grandparents so well, and feel weird not feeling as sad as they think they should.

Write down a story you want to tell about your grandma or grandpa. These are your "good words."

_____

_____

_____

_____

_____

After the Funeral

Just because the funeral is over and everybody goes home doesn't mean that your sad feelings or thoughts go away. You may feel lonely and miss the things you used to do with your grandparent. You may feel scared that somebody else you love will die. You may wonder what will happen to your grandparent now that he or she is dead.

All people on earth have bodies, with arms and legs and other parts you can see, and Christians believe that each person also has a soul, which you cannot see. The soul is the invisible part of a person that makes them who they are. Many Christians believe that even when a person has died, and the body has been buried or cremated, the person's soul is still alive in another place. We call this place heaven, and the souls there are all close to God.

It is okay to have many different feelings right now. It may have been a surprise to you that your grandparent died. Or maybe your grandparent was sick for a long time. Nothing we think about a person, or even say about them, causes them to die. Only God knows when it is someone's time to die. Those of us here on earth can always love, pray for, and talk to the people we care about, whether they are here with us, or in heaven with God.

✎ Draw a picture of heaven, as you think it would be. What colors are in heaven?

How My Grandparent Died

The first question people may ask is, "How did your grandma or grandpa die?" They are curious to know what happened. Was your grandparent sick for a long time, or for a short time? Was there an accident? What happened? If you don't know the answer, you can ask your mom or dad. If you don't understand what happened, it is okay to keep asking questions until you do.

Who told you that your grandparent died?

_____

What did that person say?

_____

_____

_____

_____

When someone dies, kids think about all sorts of things. You might wonder, "Who will die next?" You might worry about people you love dying in the future. What questions do you still have?

_____

_____

_____

_____

_____

_____

_____

_____

All of your questions are important! This could be a good time to talk to your mom or dad about your worries and questions.

My Special Remembering Prayer

Prayer is a way we talk to God. We can talk to God about the feelings that are inside of us and about what we want and hope for in our hearts. Sometimes, when we are praying to God, we feel very close to the souls of those who have died, and imagine that they can hear us too. We pray often for those who have died, because we still love them and they still love us.

When something bad happens in your life, it can be hard to make sense of it. Sometimes, we want to blame someone else for the bad things that happen. For example, we might say, "You made me spill the juice." When someone dies, we might be angry at God. We may feel that God didn't answer our prayers the way we wanted.

Even when we feel angry at God, it can be helpful to try to remember all of the good things that God has created for us in this world (just being alive, for example, or for things like blue-sky days, roller skates, ice cream, and summer vacation). Just like with our family, we can be angry at God and still love God at the same time.

What would you write if you were going to write a prayer to talk to God about your grandparent?

_____

_____

_____

_____

_____

_____

_____

_____

Be a Memory Detective

Often, lots of people come to visit after someone dies. They may come to the funeral home, to the home where your grandparent used to live, or maybe to your house. They come to let you know that they care about you and about how you are feeling now. They want to offer comfort to you and your family. They want to talk about your grandma or grandpa who died.

You may know some of the visitors. Others may be people you'll be meeting for the first time. Some will be friends of your parents. Some will be friends of your grandparents. And some will be members of your family, like aunts and uncles, or cousins.

Sometimes, a friend or relative may visit who knew your grandma or grandpa when he or she was your age. During this time, you may hear some very interesting stories about your grandparent, stories that most people have forgotten or never knew.

If you want, you can be a Memory Detective and ask people about the stories they remember. These stories are like pieces of a big puzzle that you can put together to know more about your grandparent's spirit. "Spirit" is a word that describes what made your grandparent special—how he or she acted, who he or she loved, and what was inside his or her heart.

Here are some questions that you might ask as a Memory Detective:

How did you know my grandparent?

How old were you both when you met?

What do you remember about your first meeting?

What was the most fun the two of you had together?

Did my grandma or grandpa have any special talents?

How would you describe my grandma or grandpa as a friend?

Special questions for family:

How did my grandmother and grandfather meet?

What holidays did you spend together? What kind of things did you do to celebrate?

What was my grandma like as a mother? As a wife, sister, cousin, aunt?

Or, what was my grandpa like as a father? As a husband, brother, cousin, uncle?

Write down the answers to these and other questions that you think of in the next few pages—your **Memory Detective Notebook.**

 My Memory Detective Notebook

Visitor's Name: _____

Relationship: _____

Memory Detective Report: _____

_____

_____

_____

_____

_____

Visitor's Name: _____

Relationship: _____

Memory Detective Report: _____

_____

_____

_____

_____

_____

Visitor's Name: _____

Relationship: _____

Memory Detective Report: _____

_____

_____

_____

_____

_____

 My Memory Detective Notebook

Visitor's Name: _____

Relationship: _____

Memory Detective Report: _____

_____

_____

_____

_____

_____

Visitor's Name: _____

Relationship: _____

Memory Detective Report: _____

_____

_____

_____

_____

_____

Visitor's Name: _____

Relationship: _____

Memory Detective Report: _____

_____

_____

_____

_____

_____

 My Memory Detective Notebook

Visitor's Name: _____

Relationship: _____

Memory Detective Report: _____

_____

_____

_____

_____

_____

Visitor's Name: _____

Relationship: _____

Memory Detective Report: _____

_____

_____

_____

_____

_____

Visitor's Name: _____

Relationship: _____

Memory Detective Report: _____

_____

_____

_____

_____

_____

✝

Memory Detective Biography

A biography is the story of someone's life. To write your grandparent's biography, see how many blanks you can fill in.

This is a story about my grand _____ . My grand _____ was born on _____ in _____ . (S)He was the _____ child in the family. (S)He had _____ brothers and _____ sisters. Her (His) parents were born in _____ . Her (His) mom spent her time _____ , and her (his) dad spent his time _____ .

Growing up, my grand _____ went to school at _____ . (S)He really liked to study _____ . (S)He didn't like to study _____ . My grandparents met _____ _____ and got married on _____ . They lived in _____ . They had _____ children, including _____ , my (mom)(dad), who was born on _____ . As a family, they liked to _____ . On weekends, they used to _____ . When my (mom)(dad) was growing up, (s)he thought my grand _____ was really _____ .

Since I have been in the family, my grand _____ has lived in _____ . The things I liked to do with my grand _____ were _____ and _____ . My grand _____ died on _____ .

18 ✝

Photo Memories of My Grandparent

Photographs are a wonderful way to help your memory work. When you see a photo, the picture helps you remember the people, places, and things in it. You can create a special photo album on these pages. (If you don't have a photograph for some of these memories, you can draw a picture in its place.)

My Photo Album

- Picture of your grandparent as a child or teenager
- Favorite picture of you with your grandparent
- Picture of your grandma or grandpa with your mom or dad
- Wedding picture of your grandparents
- Any other pictures you want to include

Memory Detective Hint: You can ask family friends and relatives to bring or send you photos of your grandparent. You can also ask them to tell you the story the picture shows.

✝

✝

part two

Remembering throughout the Whole Year

Even though the funeral is over, you may still have feelings about your grandparent's death. Sometimes, you may not think about what happened for days or even weeks at a time. Then suddenly, you remember, and feel all kinds of feelings. Our Christian tradition gives us special ways to remember. Here are some projects to do over the coming months and year to help you when you are thinking about your grandparent.

Names in My Family

My Name

✎ Write your name on the line below.

_____

First Name   Middle Name   Last Name

Parents give their children a name when they are born. The name can have a meaning. Daisy, for example, is a kind of flower. Or the name can be chosen in honor of someone in the family. This person might still be alive, or already have died. Sometimes, parents choose the name of a saint, like Peter or Elizabeth, or the name of a hero or heroine in the Bible, like Sarah, Joseph, or even Jesus!

How did your parents choose your name?

_____

_____

_____

If you are named after someone in your family, what can you find out about that person?

_____

_____

_____

In the Bible, people are often given names that match what they are like. For example, the angel Rafael brought healing, and his name means "healed by God." Sarah and Abraham named their son Isaac, which means "laughter," because Sarah laughed when God said she would have a baby at ninety years old!

Does your name have a special meaning? You can ask your mom or dad, or look it up in a book about names or on the computer. How are you like your name? How are you different from your name?

_____

_____

_____

24

My Grandparent's Name

 Write your grandparent's name on the line below.

_____

First Name   Middle Name   Last Name

See if you can find out the story behind your grandparent's name. Was he or she named after someone in the family?

_____

_____

My Special Name for My Grandparent

Kids have different names for their grandparents. Some people call their grandparents by their first name, Grandma Sylvia or Grandpa Jim. Other families use their own special names for the words "grandma" or "grandpa," like Grampa George, Gramma Susan, or Granny Wendy. Sometimes, families use names from another language, like *Abuelita*, which means "little grandmother" in Spanish, or *Mamgu*, which means "grandma" in Welsh. And some people make up their own names, like Poppy, PopPop, Grammie, or Nana.

There may be a family story of how your grandparent got his or her nickname. Be a Memory Detective and find out how if you can!

 Write down what you called your grandma or grandpa.

_____

Story of how my grandparent got that name:

_____

_____

When you say your grandparent's name, Katherine or James, Margaret or Thomas, do you think of your grandparent? Can you see a picture of him or her in your mind? Sometimes, people try to remember a loved one by naming a new baby after that person. When we see the new baby, and say the baby's name out loud, it helps us to remember the person who died. It's a way to keep the memory of someone you love alive. Maybe when you're older and have children of your own, you will want to name one of them after your grandmother or grandfather.

My Family Tree

On the next page is a picture of a tree. It is a special kind of tree, one that shows you how all the people in your family are related to each other. For the tree to come alive, you need to do some Memory Detective work, and fill in the branches.

Put your own name at the bottom of the page, at the place marked "me." Then see if your mom or dad, or some of the other people you speak to as a Memory Detective, can help you fill in the other branches of your family tree. You can add the names of any brothers or sisters you have. Now add your parents' names, and their brothers and sisters, who are your uncles and aunts. Now put in the children of your aunts and uncles, who are your cousins. You are doing a great job!

Now you're up to your grandparents, your mom's parents and your dad's parents. Write in their names. Here comes the harder part. Can you imagine that a very long time ago, your grandparents were babies, and they had their own mommies and daddies? These moms and dads, who were the parents of your grandparents, are called great grandparents. Can you find out the names of your great grandparents? That's going back pretty far. But maybe one of the visitors who comes to the funeral can help you with this. Maybe they even knew one of your great grandmas or great grandpas. You can also ask your mom or dad what they remember about your great grandparents. This may sound funny, but your great grandmother was your mom or dad's grandmother! Now that's something to think about!

Memory Detective Hint: Not every family tree looks the same. In families, someone may be widowed, divorced or remarried; there may be stepbrothers and stepsisters, half-brothers and half-sisters, or additional mothers or fathers (like birth mothers, when there's an adoption). Every family is different and beautiful. This tree has lots of extra spaces. You can add words or spaces so that the tree looks just like your family.

My Family Tree

Great Grandparent

Great Grandparent

Great Grandparent

Great Grandparent

Great Grandparent

Great Grandparent

Great Grandparent

Great Grandparent

Grandparent

Grandparent

Grandparent

Grandparent

Parents

Brothers & Sisters

Me

How I Am Like My Grandparent

Do people ever look at your mom or dad and say you look just like one of them? That you have your dad's eyes? Or your mom's smile?

How do you feel about that?

_____

_____

_____

_____

There are probably certain ways that you also look like your grandma or grandpa who just died. You may have the same color eyes. Or your hair may be the same color his or hers was at your age. (Hair color usually changes as we get older! Your Memory Detective talents are needed here to find out your grandparent's hair color as a child.) Maybe you can find a picture of your grandparent at a young age, and notice the ways in which you might appear similar. You might like some of the ways in which you look the same, and you may not like some of them!

Ways I look like my grandparent:

_____

_____

_____

_____

Perhaps even more importantly, there may be ways that you act like your grandparent, or maybe you have a special talent you got from him or her. For example, do you laugh like your grandma? Are you a good tennis player, like your grandpa? Do you find math really easy, like your grandmother always did? Do you have a fantastic memory, like your grandfather?

Ways I act like my grandparent:

_____

_____

_____

_____

So far, we've looked at features and talents you inherited from your grandparent, like having curly hair, or being good at drawing. You can't really choose the ways that you look like someone, or even the special talents you inherit from them. But there are other ways you can be like someone you admire or love. For example, you can volunteer to help others, as you know your grandparent did. You can read many books, just as he or she did. You can be a loyal friend. You can recycle things to help the environment. It's a very special compliment to choose to be like someone.

A way I choose to be like my grandparent:

_____

_____

_____

_____

_____

Complaints Department

This part may be a little difficult to do. When someone dies, we usually think about all the terrific things we remember about that person. However, once in a while, all of us think about things we just didn't like about someone. Sometimes, you think someone talks too loudly. You might think a person has a funny smell. Sometimes, you feel someone always criticizes you. Just like you can think about ways you want to be like your grandparent, you can also think about some ways you wouldn't want to be like him or her. This is a page for you to be able to write out your complaints. If you want it to be private, you can fold the page over when you are finished writing it.

Some things I didn't like about my grandparent:

_____

_____

_____

_____

My Grandparent's Gravestone

If your grandparent's body is buried, and often if your grandparent's body is cremated, there will be a gravestone in the cemetery to mark his or her special place. A gravestone is usually made from a big piece of rock, and words and pictures are carved into the stone. It may be there already when you go to put the coffin or box of ashes in the ground, or it may be designed and delivered to the cemetery during the months after your grandparent dies. Once the gravestone is in place, it will stay there as a permanent sign to mark the spot so you know where to go when you wish to return for a visit.

Every gravestone has a different message on it. Your grandparent's gravestone will have his or her name on it, how long he or she lived, and maybe something special he or she did while still alive. A gravestone may have words to describe the person, like "loving grandfather," or "darling wife," or "he made everyone laugh." Pictures can also be carved into the stone, showing a cross, a flower, an angel, or something else important to the person who died.

However, there may not be room to include everything you would like to remember about your grandparent on the gravestone. Using the sample here, design a gravestone on the next page for your grandparent. First, put his or her name and dates of birth and death. Then decide what other important things you want to add. See if there is a picture you want to draw, some words from the Bible or a poem you like would like to add, or a description of your grandparent in your own words.

My Design for My Grandparent's Gravestone

Visiting the Cemetery

You and your family may go to the cemetery to visit your grandparent's grave on Memorial Day, your grandparent's birthday, or any other time of year, to pray, to plant flowers, or to light a candle. At the cemetery, you can think about your grandparent, and about things you wish you could tell him or her. You can also put pretty things on the grave, like small statues or seashells.

Some cemeteries look like beautiful parks, with ponds and benches and gardens. Others are more crowded, with lots and lots of gravestones very close together. Some children feel scared going into a cemetery, and wonder if they will see ghosts, because of what they have seen on TV or read in a book. But TV and books don't always tell true stories, and you will not be seeing any ghosts at the cemetery.

Visiting your grandparent's grave can be a helpful way of remembering and loving your grandma or grandpa. It's important to know that God is as real and powerful in a cemetery as anywhere else. The Bible says, "Nothing, not death nor life … nor anything else in all Creation can separate you from the love of God" (Romans 8:38–39). This is a reminder that there is nothing to be afraid of, even in a cemetery. You can remember that the reason you are there is to show love for your grandparent and to receive love from God.

If you visited the cemetery where your grandparent is buried, how did you feel during your visit?

_____

_____

What unusual or interesting words did you find on the gravestones?

_____

_____

Did you do something to make your grandparent's gravesite more beautiful?

_____

_____

After visiting the cemetery, you might be having a lot of different thoughts. Sometimes, it's helpful to write a letter to your grandma or grandpa. If you want to, you might share your letter with your parents.

Date _____

Dear _____

There's a lot I've been thinking about since you died. Today, I went to the cemetery, and this is what I've been thinking about since then. _____

_____

_____

_____

_____

_____

_____

Love,

_____

Memory Detective Hint: If you are going to visit your grandparent's grave, take a camera with you to take a picture of the gravestone. You can glue the picture right here.

Remembering by Giving

When we give something special to someone in need, this is called giving charity. You can give money, or you can volunteer your time to help someone.

The word from the Bible that means "charity" is *caritas*, and it comes from the same word that means "caring" and "love." Jesus taught us how important it is to help others in this way. When we give charity to help people and to help the earth, we are showing how much we care about them.

Sometimes, you don't know where to offer your charity. You might think about an organization that was important to your grandparent. Maybe he or she volunteered at the local hospital, or received food from a group who delivers meals to people at home. When you give charity, you will be giving twice: honoring your grandparent, whom you are remembering, and helping the world.

Some Addresses for Giving to Charity

To help poor people have new houses:
Habitat for Humanity
121 Habitat Street
Americus, GA 31709
www.habitat.org

To help poor families raise animals, grow food, and plant trees:
Heifer Project International
P.O. Box 8058
Little Rock, AR 72203
www.heifer.org

To give wheelchairs to those in need:
The Free Wheelchair Mission
P.O. Box 513538
Los Angeles, CA 90051
www.freewheelchairmission.org

To help children who are ill:
Locks of Love
2925 10th Avenue North, Ste. 102
Lake Worth, FL 33461
www.locksoflove.org

To help families in emergencies:
Church World Service
28606 Phillips Street
P.O. Box 968
Elkhart, IN 46515
www.churchworldservice.org

To give food to people who are starving:
Bread for the World
50 F Street, NW, Ste. 500
Washington, D.C. 20001
www.bread.org

Where did you choose to send money? Is this something your grandparent did, or was it your own idea?

Even if you don't have a lot of money, there are other ways to give that mean just as much.

Some Additional Things You Can Do to Help Others

- You can visit old people in a senior center or assisted living center and play games, play a musical instrument, sing songs, or read a story.
- You can serve food at a homeless shelter. You could also bring food you have cooked to the shelter for the people there to eat.
- You can collect toys and art supplies for poor children.
- You can clean up a park or another outdoor space, or plant trees in a city neighborhood.

In churches and out in the world, you may have heard the phrase "eternal life." What does this mean? Partly, it means the kind of life that your grandparent, and anyone else who dies, goes on to have in heaven. But it also means that the kind of life he or she had keeps living on in you and the things you do. Whenever you carry on traditions that were important to your grandparent, like volunteering or giving to charity, you are part of making your grandparent's "eternal life" come true.

What volunteer work did you choose to do?

_____

How did helping others make you feel? Would you do it again?

_____

_____

When you send money to an organization, or do volunteer work, you can let them know that you are thinking about your grandparent who died. Usually, the organization will send you a thank you note. You can put it on this page.

You can put a thank you note here.

Memory Detective Mind Benders

With all you have discovered about your grandparent in your detective work, try to complete the following sentences.

My favorite time with my grandparent was _____

_____

Having my grandparent die makes me think about _____

_____

I loved it when my grandparent _____

_____

If I could have one thing that belonged to my grandparent, I would choose _____

_____

The way my mom or dad is just like my grandparent is _____

_____

Since my grandparent died, I sometimes worry about _____

_____

The one thing I wish my grandparent could do with me now is _____

_____

The one thing I'm most upset about my grandparent not being able to do with me is

_____

My grandparent taught me something about _____

_____

When I'm a grandparent, I would like to _____

_____

Something my grandparent always used to say was _____

_____

part three

Remembering during the Holidays

Celebrating the holidays can be fun. We do special things for each holiday, like decorating a tree at Christmas and coloring eggs at Easter. Holiday times can make us feel closer to our families. But we might also feel sad when we remember and miss people we love who have died. Here are some ideas to keep the memory of your grandparent alive as part of your holiday celebrations.

Christmas

Christmas is special because it is the birthday of Jesus.

Christmas is also the time for giving gifts. We give gifts to each other to remind ourselves of how the Wise Men traveled a long way just to meet and give gifts to the baby Jesus. They knew how important he was, and we give gifts to show how important our families are to us.

Think about a special present you got in the past from your grandparent. Was it a bicycle, a book, a computer program?

A Christmas present from my grandparent:

_____

_____

_____

Now think again. Your grandparent may have given you another kind of gift, one that cannot be bought in a store. For example, maybe your grandma taught you something, like how to play checkers. Or maybe you and your grandpa had a fun day at the beach together. Or maybe there was a favorite song, or story, or way that they hugged you, or understood how you felt when you were sad. See if you can remember a special gift that you got from your grandparent. This gift is one that you can't touch and that you can't buy in a store, but one that you can keep in your heart.

A special gift from my grandparent that I can't buy in a store:

_____

_____

_____

The Taste of Christmas

Often, we remember sharing good times with people at holiday meals and celebrations we had together. Maybe you remember your grandpa's special "Chicken à la Grandpa," or your grandma's famous spaghetti with tomato sauce. Was there something special that your grandparent made for Christmas? Did you bake Christmas cookies with your grandma, or make pancakes Christmas morning with your grandpa?

See if you can get the recipe for one or two of your favorite dishes that your grandma or grandpa made. You can try to make them by yourself, or maybe your mom or dad will help you. In any case, when you make the recipe, and then again when you eat it, have a special thought about your grandparent. This is the secret ingredient that will make it taste as delicious as when your grandma or grandpa made it.

My special recipe for: _____

Ingredients: _____

_____

_____

_____

Directions: _____

_____

_____

_____

My memories of my grandma or grandpa making this recipe:

_____

_____

_____

Memory Detective Note: Maybe your grandparent didn't cook at all. But he or she may have taken you out to a restaurant, or maybe to a bakery to get a cupcake or a cookie. You can write down something that you liked eating when you were together, and then, with some help, you can find a recipe for that food.

Ash Wednesday

Ash Wednesday is a quiet holiday in the Christian church that comes between Christmas and Easter. It is a time for thinking about the things that have happened during the past year, and about what we may have done wrong.

You may go to church on Ash Wednesday to say prayers, sing songs, and receive ashes in the shape of a cross on your forehead. The ashes for Ash Wednesday are made by burning the palm branches that were waved in church on Palm Sunday the previous year. Palm Sunday is a day of celebration, a day for parades and singing and thinking about life, not death. So the ashes we put on our foreheads remind us of this cycle: that death is a part of life, and life a part of death.

On Ash Wednesday, we think about our lives over the past year. Something we might think about is how we have treated other people. Almost everyone can think of something they wish they had done a little differently. Perhaps you wish you had called your grandma or grandpa on the telephone more often. You think of things you wish you had said or done, but now it seems too late. This can be pretty upsetting for kids and adults alike. One of the hardest things in life is feeling like we acted badly toward someone who died before we had a chance to say we're sorry.

It's important to know that almost everyone has feelings like that. Nobody is perfect as a son or daughter, as a grandson or granddaughter, or even as a mom or dad, grandma or grandpa. Still, it's important to have a chance to think about your behavior, and make plans for changing it in the future. Here are some ideas, step by step:

✎ Write a list of things you may have done wrong or things for which you would like to apologize to your grandparent. Some may be little things. Some may seem like big things.

Things I'm sorry about:

A. _____

B. _____

C. _____

For each item on the list, see if you can figure out why you acted the way you did. For example, if you didn't call your grandmother as much as you think you should have, was there some reason? Maybe you found it hard to talk to her? Maybe you thought she criticized you a lot? Talk to your parents. They can probably tell you something about your grandparent that will help you to understand your feelings and actions.

Why I acted that way:

A. _____

B. _____

C. _____

All of us know of things we have done in the past year that we don't like very much. We were mean to our sister or brother. We were grumpy with our parents. We left out a friend. On Ash Wednesday we think about these actions, and we also get a chance to do something about them.

At the worship service, we will say a prayer of confession. It might not say all the things you have done wrong, but you can say those extra things in your heart during the moments of silence, and God will hear them. In this prayer, we can get rid of all the bad things we have done. And with them, we get rid of all the bad feelings that go with them. Once we have admitted we did something wrong, it's easier to believe that God forgives us. We will probably feel better as soon as we've told God what we feel bad about—that is God's forgiveness already at work in us.

Then you will walk up to the front of the church and the minister or priest will put the shape of a cross on your forehead with ashes. This is to help you know that God has forgiven you—the ashes are a symbol that God has cleaned all the bad feelings and actions out of you.

Goodbye, goodbye to those things!

Now you are ready to have a fresh start,

and do the good things that God wants you to do!

Memory Detective Note: Did you know that ashes used to be one of the main ingredients in soap? So when you get ashes on your forehead, even though it may look dirty, it is actually like "cleaning" yourself with old-fashioned soap!

Easter

Easter is the most important Christian holiday. Does that surprise you? It is the time we remember the saddest and happiest part of the story of Jesus, the son of God. Jesus was born as a baby and lived as a man, healing and teaching and loving all people. But then he died in a painful way. This is the sad part. The story continues that Jesus was resurrected from the dead—this means that after he died and his friends had buried him, he came alive again by the power of God. He went to visit his friends one by one, and they were amazed and very happy to see him. This was a miracle from God. Today, we don't know of any people who came alive again like Jesus did.

This story teaches us that sometimes things have to die before other things can be born. Every year when winter comes, the plants in our gardens die. But the old plants get made into healthy soil that helps to feed the new seeds we plant the following spring. Even when the people we love die, the death of their bodies can teach us something new about ourselves and the good things we are made of. New life can come out of death—this is what Easter is all about.

What is a way that you have changed since your grandparent died? Have you grown an inch, started a new school, or made a new friend?

_____

_____

_____

Any time someone you love dies, you change, and become a little more grown up. What new things have you learned since your grandparent died?

_____

_____

_____

_____

Vacation

Vacations are fun times when you don't have to go to school, your parents don't have to go to work, and you get to have fun and spend time together as a family. Many families go on a vacation during the summer, but you can go any time of the year. Maybe you enjoyed some vacations with your grandparent before he or she died. Did your grandparent fly in an airplane to your house, or did you drive in a car to visit him or her, or did you meet somewhere in between? Did you live in the same city or town, and go together to another place, like the beach?

Did you go camping by a lake, or check out museums in the city with your grandparent? Did you go fishing, or take a cruise, or just sit on the porch together as the sun set? (It counts as a vacation, even if your grandparent came to visit you at your house!)

Write down one memory you have of a vacation you took with your grandparent. You can write about something fun that you did, something you ate, or something wonderful that you saw or learned.

_____

_____

This year, when you go on vacation, you may miss your grandparent, and wish that he or she could be with you. Write what you think your grandparent would have liked best about your vacation (or if you think your grandparent wouldn't have liked it, you can write about that!).

_____

_____

Memory Detective: To the right is a blank map. You can draw in flags like the one below for the place where you live, where your grandparent lived, and for all the places you spent time together on vacation.

If you want, you can draw your flags to look like this:

All Saints' Day and Día de los Muertos

Everyone knows about Halloween, but do you know what holiday Christians celebrate on the day after Halloween? November 1 is All Saints' Day, a day when we pray for all those who have died and celebrate special servants of God, whom we call the "saints."

Some children think of Halloween as a time to be scared of the dead. All Saints' Day is just the opposite. It is a time to realize that people who have died have not become something scary and cannot hurt us. Even though we can't see or touch people who have died, they are still with us in a loving way. Everybody and everything belong to God and to God's world. We are never really separated, even if we feel like we are.

In Mexico, Christians celebrate All Saints' Day in a special way they call Day of the Dead (Día de los Muertos). They are not afraid of death, but believe that those who have died have a different kind of life, one that we can only imagine in our minds. On Día de los Muertos, Mexican families create little decorated tables, called altars, celebrating the lives of people they love who have died. On these tables they gather flowers, fruit, candles, favorite foods of the dead person, family pictures and treasures that belonged to them, as well as sweet breads and *papel picado* (tissue paper with special cutout designs).

On Day of the Dead, many Mexican families will go to the local cemetery and have a picnic in front of the gravestones of people they love! This may seem strange to us, but it is a way for them to keep feeling close to those who have died.

Memory Detective Hint: To make *papel picado*, you can take one piece of regular paper, and put three or four sheets of colored tissue paper on top of it. Fold the paper in half, and then in half again. You can then cut out shapes to make a design, like a snowflake or a flower.

If you want, you and your parents can make a Day of the Dead altar for your grandparent in a room in your house, or you can draw one on a piece of paper. Don't forget to include your grandparent's favorite foods, pictures of your grandparent, beautiful flowers, and *papel picado*. You can tape your picture onto this page.

Thanksgiving

 Thanksgiving is a time for families to be together to give thanks to God for life, for health, and for having each other. It is also a chance to eat until we feel we could burst!

Thanksgiving was first celebrated by a group of Christians, called Pilgrims, who came to this land a long time ago and who were thankful to have enough to eat at harvest time. Eventually, Thanksgiving became a national holiday celebrated not just by Christians, but by people of every religion and no religion. It is still a time to give thanks for what we have, whether it is a little or a lot, and to say "thank you" to all who have helped give us what we need to live well.

The holidays can be fun, but they can also feel strange or sad if you are missing someone you usually see. It can feel like there is an empty place at the table when you sit down and don't see your grandparent's face. Even if your grandparent died a while ago, you may miss special things about them. The way your grandpa carved the turkey. The chocolate fudge pecan pie that your grandma always made. Here is an activity you can do to remember your grandparent at the Thanksgiving feast.

Write a prayer of thanksgiving talking to God and naming all the things that make you feel glad to be alive. At the end of your prayer, add one thing you are glad to have done with your grandparent when he or she was alive. If you would like to, ask your mom or dad if you could say your prayer at the table before everyone eats. After you read your prayer, invite everyone else around the dinner table to name one thing he or she is thankful for, and then have everyone shout loudly at the end: AMEN!

My prayer of thanksgiving:

_____

_____

_____

_____

Memory Detective Activity: Create a place card for everyone who will be at your Thanksgiving meal. Put the person's name and a special decoration (like a heart, a book, a flower, or a cat) on the place card. Now make a place card for your grandparent who died. Even though he or she won't be sitting with you at the table this year, you can put the place card on the table to help everyone remember your grandparent's spirit.

Remembering My Grandparent in the Circle of Life

This circle stands for the earth, which keeps turning around and around every day of the week, month after month, year after year. As time goes on, our feelings may also go around. Sometimes, memories that used to make us feel sad now bring us happiness.

Everything has its season, and there is a time for every thing ... Everything has its season, and there is a time for every thing ... be sad and a time to dance ... (Ecclesiastes 3:1–2, 4)

under the heavens. A time to be born and a time to die.... A time to cry and a time to laugh.... A time to

Inside this circle, you can make a collage celebrating your grandparent's life. You can draw, paint, cut out pictures or words from magazines, paste in photographs, pieces of ribbon, wrapping paper, or any other materials you can think of.

Glossary

Cemetery: Special place, often filled with trees and flowers, where either the bodies or the ashes of dead people are buried.

Charity (*caritas*): Helping someone else, either by volunteering or by giving money.

Coffin: Special, large box, which looks a little like a bed, in which the body of a dead person is buried.

Cremation: Turning the body of a dead person into ashes, using a special fire.

Eternal life: The way we live with God after we die, which lasts forever.

Eulogy: The stories and "good words" told about a person's life at the funeral, by a minister, a priest, family, and friends.

Funeral: Special service where ministers or priests, friends and family, get together to pray and tell stories about a person who died.

Gravestone: A piece of rock sculpture in a cemetery that marks the place of a grave and has writing carved into it to identify who is buried at that place.

Grief: Feelings of sadness, anger, and missing someone terribly, usually after someone you love dies.

Heaven: A beautiful place without tears or pain, where we imagine that souls go to live with God after death.

Resurrection: The act of coming alive again, by the power of God, after death.

Soul: The invisible, innermost part of a person that makes a person unique, and that stays alive even after the body dies.

Wake: Time in the days before the funeral when family and friends come to the funeral home and see the body of the dead person, all dressed up, lying in the coffin; also called a "viewing" or "visiting hours."

A Note to Kids Who Used This Book from the Authors Who Wrote It

We started this book, but you finished it! By working on this book, you have joined us to become one of its authors. It is different from any other book because you wrote it about yourself and your grandparent!

We wrote this book for kids like you, and we would love to hear from you about your feelings and ideas. We would enjoy seeing photocopies of how your pictures, prayers, and other creations turned out.

If you have some favorite pages from the book, we would be very happy if you would make copies, and mail them to us at this address:

Nechama Liss-Levinson and Molly Phinney Baskette
c/o SkyLight Paths Publishing
P.O. Box 237
Woodstock, VT 05091

9 781683 362593